Ben Lowe is author of a book on NATO published in Spain as part of the campaign for Spanish withdrawal during the referendum of March 1986, *La Cara Oculta de la OTAN;* a contributor to *Mad Dogs* edited by Edward Thompson and Mary Kaldor; and a member of the Socialist Society, which has provided financial and research support for this pamphlet.

Ben Lowe

Peace through Non-Alignment

The Case Against British Membership of NATO

The Campaign Group of Labour MPs
welcomes the publication of this pamphlet and
believes that the arguments it contains are worthy
of serious consideration.

VERSO
The Imprint of New Left Books

First published 1986
Verso Editions & NLB
15 Greek St, London W1
© Ben Lowe 1986
ISBN 086091882
Typeset by Red Lion Setters
86 Riversdale Road, N5

Printed and bound by
CPI Group (UK) Ltd,
Croydon, CR0 4YY

Contents

Foreword

This pamphlet, which argues the case for Britain to leave NATO and move towards a non-aligned foreign and defence policy, has been very widely discussed. Those of us who are sponsoring it belive that the information it contains, and the conclusions that it reaches, are of the greatest importance and ought to be made publicly available.

We also know very well that successive Labour Party conferences, and election manifestoes, have committed Labour governments to retain British membership of NATO. When the general election comes, all of us who are parliamentary candidates will, quite rightly, be explaining to our electors that this is the official policy of the party.

Nevertheless, there are many people, both inside and outside the Party, who most certainly do want to see the issue raised, as became apparent at the 1985 Labour Conference when nearly 2½ million votes were actually cast for a resolution asking the NEC to re-examine Britain's NATO membership.

This is partly because there is a clear potential contradiction between Labour's commitment to NATO, and its equally clear commitment to the removal of all nuclear weapons and US nuclear bases from Britain. For if the American government refuses to accede to that demand and threatens to end our NATO membership if we persist, a stark choice may have to be made. In New Zealand a Labour government, backed up by a solid majority of electoral support, has also had to face outright opposition from the Americans, who are effectively squeezing New Zealand out of the ANZUS treaty.

Furthermore, President Reagan's decision to bomb Libya from US bases in Britain shows that the country is now seen in Washington as an unsinkable aircraft carrier—a thought that cannot be very reassuring to British people who are at risk whenever it is used for that purpose.

It was after the war, at about the time that NATO was formed, that Mr Attlee agreed that some US aircraft should come to Britain on 'training missions'. From then on, the US presence has grown substantially and become permanent, until today it totals about 130 bases or installations and about 30,000 service personnel. The agreement under which they operate here has never been published, and it is not even clear whether any treaty regulations exist. The most likely estimate is that there is an informal understanding under which successive Prime Ministers have agreed with successive Presidents that US forces will not be used without a measure of consultation, though exactly what that would mean, or how it would be conducted, has never been clear.

According to the oath of office which confers upon every American President duties as Commander-in-Chief of all US Forces worldwide, the US Constitution would not permit him to subordinate his military powers and responsibilities to the wishes of any foreign power, however friendly. Legislation recently introduced into Congress would actually absolve him from his present requirement to consult Congress before taking action against so-called terrorist attacks, and no British Prime Minister could expect to be put in a more advantageous position that the US legislature itself.

Thus it would appear that the theory of a British veto is an illusion—the United States has the right, as well as the power, to use its bases in Britain as it wishes, either for NATO purposes, or in pursuit of its own world-wide interests.

Recently it has become known that the British government has even prepared plans that would transfer great powers to the US military over whole areas of our own country, in the event of war.

Despite the oft-repeated argument that the United States is solely concerned to protect freedom, human rights and democracy, it has actually built up a vast World Empire, far more powerful even than the old British Empire, with 3000 bases scattered across the globe to defend US economic and political interests including her investments, raw material supplies, especially oil, and the markets for her goods. In defence of those interests America has fought a long war in Vietnam, attacked Cuba, occupied Grenada, destabilized Chile and organized terrorist attacks gainst Nicaragua, as well as propping up some of the most corrupt and dictatorial regimes of the twentieth century.

Given these indisputable facts it cannot be right, or safe, for Britain to continue to allow the United States to use military bases in our country to pursue those policies.

All these developments have been noticed by a large number of British people who would not regard themselves as in any way anti-American, who remember the US help during the last war, and who admire the courage of those Americans who have fought so hard against the Vietnam war, for Civil Rights and Peace, and against the aggressive policies of the Reagan administration in Central America.

In recent months, indeed, there has developed widespread opposition both within the United States itself and throughout Western Europe to the so-called Strategic Defence Initiative of the White House. The launching of the criminally wasteful Star Wars project, when millions die each year in the Third World for lack of the simple technologies and amenities which that money could be used to buy, has alerted the British people to the urgent need for new initiatives by our own government.

There is another reason why opinion in Britain is shifting rapidly away from the present subservience to Washington, and it has come into focus since the tragic disaster at Chernobyl. It must now be clear that even if no nuclear attack was ever made against this country itself, Britain and Europe would suffer terrible losses as a result of any nuclear weapons launched by NATO onto Warsaw Pact countries, while the USA could rely upon the Atlantic Ocean to protect its own people from contamination.

All these developments together point towards the adoption by the Labour Party of a non-aligned foreign policy: working for detente and co-operation between the super-powers; a massive reduction of Britain's own high defence expenditure; and a re-direction of the money thus released, to meet the urgent needs of working people here and world-wide and to restore full employment in Britain.

We are often told to face the harsh realities—however unpleasant that may be—and the harsh reality is that Lbour's long-established advocacy of the American alliance, and the existence of US bases in Britain, no longer meets the needs or aspirations of the people of this country. A clear policy commitment to close all US bases in Britain as soon as Labour returns to power, if honestly presented and strongly pressed, would undoubtedly receive very widespread support far beyond the ranks of the party and its traditional voters.

We hope that every constituency party and affiliated trade union will arrange conferences and seminars to discuss this pamphlet, and that all those organizations that are working in any way for detente, disarmament and development will read it too and have the question of NATO put upon their own agenda. The launching in July 1986, at the House of Commons, of a new movement to promote the idea of non-alignment for Britain, and the warm welcome it received from many such organizations, indicate something of the range of support it already enjoys.

We believe that as time passes, support for this policy will grow until it wins a majority inside the Labour Party—just as unilateralism has done over the last twenty-five years—and that the electors, as a whole, will also come to see that non-alignment offers a constructive alternative for Britain to adopt.

Tony Benn and Jeremy Corbyn
September 1986

Introduction

Britain has been a member of the North Atlantic Treaty Organization since it was founded thirty-seven years ago. For most of this period the Labour Party, whether in government or in opposition, loyally supported the military and political initiatives radiating from the Washington hub of the Alliance. Although forces on the left at times campaigned against such policies and practices, Labour foreign secretaries and defence spokesmen eagerly helped to build a pro-NATO consensus that mirrored the Butskellism of internal British politics, often outvying the Tories in enthusiasm for the 'special relationship' with the United States. In recent years, this old orthodoxy has begun to give way before a wide-ranging debate which has focused particularly on Britain's own nuclear weapons and on the US military presence in this country. In large measure, this change has been part of a wider European trend, as peace movements and a number of Socialist parties have expressed alarm at the new belligerence of the NATO high command. Whereas, in the Cold War of the fifties, Washington and its European allies successfully manipulated the Red Scare to line up a major part of the non-Communist electorate, today the fear of American power and intentions is a potent factor in many countries of Western Europe. In Greece and Denmark, even the governments have broken ranks on important Alliance decisions.

The country where the most fundamental questions have been raised about the Atlantic Alliance is Spain. In 1982, when the Socialist Party took office, it was committed to a referendum on NATO membership and had played a leading role in a campaign to withdraw Spain from the Alliance. Four years later, when the referendum was finally held, the government found itself arguing the opposite position and only just managed to carry a majority of the electorate with it. Yet issues had entered the public arena that had effectively been closed from most NATO countries since 1949. Why be a member of NATO? What were the real reasons for its formation? Does the Alliance have any commitment to principles of freedom and democracy? Is there really a Soviet military threat? Does it make a country safer to be neutral rather than in NATO? In this pamphlet, we argue that such questions must be posed for Britain too.

1

In fact, there is already a widespread perception that subservience to the United States is undermining the security of the British people. This perception has become firmer in the wake of the Westland affair, the furore over the selling off of Landrover and Leyland, the bullying of peace protesters at US bases, Thatcher's decision to allow US aircraft to stage their attack on Libya from Britain, and her sheep-like following of President Reagan on such issues as Star Wars or membership of UNESCO. In a poll conducted in April 1986, forty-nine per cent of respondents considered the 'special relationship' with America to be 'harmful', against a mere thirty-nine per cent who regarded it as 'helpful'.[1] At the same time, dissident voices have begun to appear on the fringes of the military establishment: the most eloquent is former British Air Attaché Peter Johnson, who argued recently that Britain will only find 'security and self-respect' in neutrality and that withdrawal from NATO would lead to 'an active and positive role in the world which would be a tonic for our ailing country'.[2] From their own point of view, leading Tories are also questioning the future viability of the Alliance, and ministers involved in the decision to purchase Trident submarines have privately confided that it was in part a safeguard against US withdrawal from Europe.

It is high time that the Labour movement, instead of lagging behind in the strategic debate, should move beyond a revision of specific nuclear policies and look hard at the very structures of Cold War, the military blocs tht fuel tension between East and West, and the new system of international relations that a Labour government should seek to promote. It is the purpose of this pamphlet to encourage debate on these and related matters. Part One examines the origins and *raison d'être* of NATO, its role in US foreign policy, its nuclear strategies and its effect on British politics and national security. An alternative perspective on NATO history and East-West relations is, in our view, necessary for serious campaigning work, and any new approach to the Eastern bloc must break down the Cold War images that are constantly reproduced by the Atlantic Alliance. Part Two discusses whether Labour's anti-nuclear policy is consistent with membership of NATO, and how NATO itself would be likely to relate to a Labour government that attempted to implement its programme. That we are not alone in questioning the coherence of Labour's present position was demonstrated by the Shadow Foreign Secretary at a recent Party conference. For our part, however, we argue that withdrawal from NATO is the logical conclusion to Labour's review of foreign and defence policy. It is also the only way in which Labour can escape the Cold War dragnet and actively contribute to a new process of genuine detente.

Part one:
NATO and the Post-War World

Origins of the Alliance

Britain played a key role in the creation of NATO, building on the Atlantic Charter and the various agreements reached with the United States during the Second World War. Ernest Bevin, foreign secretary in the post-war Labour government, consciously followed the basic policy of his wartime colleague and Tory counterpart, Anthony Eden: namely, to solicit American aid in propping up its world position as an imperial power. In return, the United States would gain the use of military bases in the UK and share the benefits of many of Britain's overseas bases and colonies.[3] The idea of extending this alliance was first raised by British and US officials in the fateful autumn of 1947, when the Western powers decided to press ahead with the division of Germany even if this should worsen tensions with the Soviet Union. Already in June, however, Washington had tabled the so-called Marshall Plan: an offer of millions of dollars in aid to investment-starved Europe, which would serve to establish an inter-dependent Atlantic system providing new capital outlets and trade patterns for the US economy. When, under pressure from Moscow, East European leaders refused to open their national books wide to Wall Street—as the Marshall Plan required—the project followed its intended course of integrating Western Germany into a US-dominated bloc and accelerating the division of the European continent. At the same time, Marshall Aid allowed the Americans to apply a direct and powerful lever in the post-war recomposition of West European politics. Until 1947 a number of West European Communist Parties occupied a central, and recognized, position in national political life—above all, in Italy and France—just as right-wing politicians often participated in government in Eastern Europe. As Marshall made clear to the Italian premier in May, however—a month before the Plan was announced—American aid was contingent on the removal of Communists from governmental office.[1] It would take only a matter of months for Western Europe's

3

Communists to be driven into the ghetto, in preparation for the headlong rush into Cold War regimentation of the non-Communist labour movement.

The formation of a military alliance was a natural component of the new Atlantic order. Shortly after the US Congress approved Marshall Aid in early 1948, secret discussions began on NATO among British, American and Canadian officials—the venue, appropriately enough, being the Pentagon War Room.[5] The documents which emerged from these talks had evidently passed through the skilful hands of professional civil servants. Article Four, for instance, blandly states: 'The Parties will consult together whenever . . . the territorial integrity, political independence or security of any of the Parties is threatened.' Behind the closed doors of the War Room, the Americans made it clear that they wanted the right to intervene, through economic and diplomatic measures and low-grade military operations, in the event of any 'political change favourable to an aggressor'— which could easily be interpreted to apply to an electoral victory by Communists or radical Socialists.[6] In any case, the Americans went ahead and prepared plans to intervene in such countries as Italy and France, and no doubt they would have carried them out if the need had arisen.

Soviet leaders reacted to these moves with a mixture of belligerent rhetoric and acts of repression in Eastern Europe. Eventually the first full-blown crisis in East-West relations erupted in 1948, when Moscow sought to hinder Anglo-US plans for Western Germany by blockading the West Berlin enclave within the Soviet-controlled zone. In the course of the next year, the American airlift and the accompanying ideological offensive completed the isolation of those European political parties and trade unions which were opposed to the idea of NATO. When ratification of the Atlantic Treaty was sought in mid-1949, a parliamentary majority was secured in all twelve founder countries. A few months later, the Federal Republic of Germany came into existence at the heart of Europe, held together by the cement of anti-Communism in both its internal and its external relations.

The Berlin crisis also provided the occasion for the establishment of the first nuclear bases in Britain and Western Germany—without any written agreement or regulations—and for the first nuclear threats and contingency plans against the Soviet Union.[7] Britain, for its part, had already launched a nuclear programme of its own, following a secret decision by a group of Labour ministers and right-wing officials in 1947. But the object of Western threats—the USSR—only succeeded in developing the atom bomb around the time that the NATO treaty came into effect, in August 1949.

4

Until then, and for a short period after, US confidence was so high and hawkishness so rampant that serious consideration was given to the use of bases in Europe and elsewhere to 'roll back' the Soviet presence in Eastern Europe.[8]

The Korean War of 1950-53, in which the Americans actively sought to 'roll back' at least one Communist gain, generated such a level of hysteria that Western leaders pressed on to turn NATO into a fully fledged military structure, with its own operational headquarters (initially in France, then in Belgium), a single command and a Supreme Commander who was always to be an American. The first was Dwight D. Eisenhower. A year after the end of the Korean War, the French government finally agreed to West Germany's rearmament and its accession to NATO. Early in 1955, once the division of Germany had been sealed in this way, the Soviet bloc responded by forming the Warsaw Pact as a rival to NATO.

America's Global Order

According to the annual statement of the US Defense Secretary, NATO is America's major 'foreign policy commitment'. This simple assertion, revealing in its linkage of foreign and military policy, raises the question of how NATO fits into US global strategy. A few years ago, the prestigious magazine *Business Week* described in a major feature how, from 1944, 'the US deliberately constructed out of the ruins of the war an international monetary order based on the dollar.... With its nuclear umbrella and armed forces, the US stood ready to guarantee this open economic system against threats from the Soviet Union on the outside and enemies that might close off certain markets and needed resources such as oil on the inside. As both banker and cop, the US was the guarantor of the postwar global economy.'[9]

The self-appointed role of global policeman had several ramifications: it required allies, to compensate for America's limited military resources; it involved huge increases in US military spending; and it implied a willingness, at times, to adopt the role of soldier, with aggressive intent in relation to perceived enemies—not least the Soviet Union and radical nationalist movements. NATO not only provided the structure through which the United States could up to a point ensure that anti-capitalist forces were kept from power in Western Europe, but also created a powerful bond within the Atlantic system vis-à-vis the Third World. Of course the interests of the United States did not always coincide with those of the old European colonial powers: the sharpest clash occurred over the Anglo-French-Israeli invasion of Suez in 1956, when Washington's lack of support sufficed to cool the militarist ardour in a matter of days. But for much of NATO's early life, Britain, France and Portugal received enthusiastic US backing for their colonial wars in Asia and Africa. When the Labour Government finally considered withdrawing from East of Suez in the mid-1960s, the US Defense Secretary reportedly told his British counterpart, Denis Healey, that the United States wanted Britain to keep a foothold in Hong Kong, Malaya and the Persian Gulf, 'to enable us to do things for the Alliance which they can't do'. The forces there were 'much more useful to the Alliance outside Europe'.[10]

France committed a huge part of its armed forces to the war in Indochina in the early 1950s, and towards the end was receiving eighty per cent of the necessary funds from the United States. It was fully in line with US policy that the NATO Council passed a resolution in 1952 to the effect that 'the campaign being led by the forces of the Union Française in Indochina deserves the unrestricted support of the Atlantic governments'.[11] After the French defeat in 1954, Washington stepped in to create a formal alliance— the so-called South-East Asia Treaty Organization—which actually comprised one South-East Asian state, Thailand, together with the USA, Britain, France, Pakistan and three Pacific countries. The long, savage war against Vietnam's national liberation forces was to be its most bitter fruit.

It is perhaps less well known that Portugal's wars in sub-Saharan Africa, starting in the early 1960s, were mainly fought with NATO equipment, despite the objections of Scandinavian members of the Alliance.[12] The US Assistant Secretary of State for Africa explained in 1963 that 'it is neither in our interest to see the Portuguese leave Africa, nor to curtail their influence there'[13]—a policy refined still further with Nixon's commitment to preserve 'economic, scientific and strategic interests in the white states' of southern Africa, while expanding 'opportunities for profitable trade and investment'.[14] The British Tories followed suit, even trying to extend the ambit of NATO to include South Africa, its white-ruled neighbours and the Southern Atlantic. Thus Geoffrey Rippon, MP, then a minister, told the House of Commons in 1970 that 'NATO should broaden its maritime horizons . . . . The South Atlantic should now be included to give support and backing to our Portuguese allies against the spread of communism in Africa.'[15]

As far as America's own military operations are concerned, its bases in the NATO area furnish an invaluable springboard to North Africa, the Middle East and the Persian Gulf—as when US forces moved into Lebanon in 1958 to prop up a pro-American government, or, more recently, when the F1-11s set off on their bombing raid on Libya. During the Lebanon intervention, US nuclear weapons targeted on the Soviet Union were placed on alert, in order to 'keep Moscow at bay'—a role which, as we shall see, was repeated in the international crises of 1962 and 1973. Such manoeuvres place Europe in the front line in any confrontation between East and West, or between the United States and its foes in many parts of the world. Nor is this all. We should now turn to the long-standing plans within NATO to use nuclear weapons to strike against the Communist regime in the Soviet Union.

NATO's Nuclear Strategies

NATO's strategic nuclear weapons are overwhelmingly in the hands of the Americans. The US President has the final say over their use, and it is US officials who negotiate with the Russians over how or how not to limit their production. Not surprisingly, therefore, NATO's nuclear doctrines also originate in the United States. The first of these, introduced in 1954, involved the deliberately unambiguous concept of 'massive retaliation', whereby the most powerful weapons would be used at the outset of a conflict. President Eisenhower justified this policy by stating that the administration wished to avoid a repetition of the Korean War, in which the US armed forces became bogged down for three long years.[16] Faced with the threat of immediate nuclear attack, it was felt, any adversary would back down without a fight. In line with such thinking, Washington came close to using nuclear weapons on a number of occasions—in Guatemala and Vietnam in 1954, in China, Lebanon and Jordan in 1958, in Berlin in 1959, and in Laos in 1960.[17] In the same period, some seven thousand 'tactical' nuclear weapons became the spearhead of NATO's 'forward strategy' in Europe, which kept open the possibility of a lower-level nuclear response even in the event of, say, an uprising in Eastern Europe that the US might wish to encourage. NATO claimed that this build-up was required to offset Soviet superiority in conventional forces, but in reality the Pentagon's constant aim was to turn any battle into a nuclear conflict—or at least to have this as an option.[18]

The US armed forces, particularly the Army, turned against 'massive retaliation' in the late 1950s because they felt that fear of all-out nuclear war might weaken the political will to intervene militarily when US interests appeared to be under threat. The Kennedy Administration accordingly introduced a new strategy of 'flexible response' in 1961 which, by laying greater stress on conventional forces, was supposed to enhance the capacity to fight wars 'without going nuclear'.[19] It was this interventionist impulse underlying 'flexible response' that was soon to take the United States into its catastrophic war against Vietnam.

West European leaders initially opposed the new doctrine, seeing the reluctance to use nuclear weapons at once as a sign of flagging US resolve to defend Europe in a crisis. But 'flexible response' was dressed up to appear almost the same as its predecessor, and it became official NATO policy in 1967. At that time, the escalating US commitment to the war in Vietnam anyway precluded greater reliance on conventional weapons in Europe. Even in the early 1980s, NATO's war-planning envisaged the use of nuclear weapons in less than four days after the outbreak of war—one of the reasons being that much of NATO's tactical weaponry is deployed very close to Warsaw Pact borders. Moreover, the NATO commanders' fear that the Russians might gain an edge by taking the nuclear initiative—a clear case of projecting one's own ambitions onto the 'enemy'—has dominated military thinking throughout the nuclear era and fostered a 'first use' mentality which is not mirrored in the Warsaw Pact.[20]

The turn to 'flexible response' in the 1960s coincided with a period in which the Soviet Union was approaching rough strategic equality with the United States. It was thus recognized by the US military that the destruction of each side was assured in the event of full-scale conflict—hence the phrase 'mutually assured destruction' (MAD). This concept was used to justify the continued mass production of nuclear weapons. According to MAD, there had to be sufficient weapons, but no more, for each force (Air Force, Navy, Army) to kill a third of the Soviet population and destroy a third of its industry. Moscow and Washington then began to negotiate increases or improvements in their respective armouries so as to maintain 'assured destruction' at an unacceptable level. This was called arms control.

It would be wrong to think, however, that the MAD guidelines ever supplanted the idea of 'limited nuclear war' in Europe. In fact, the contingency plans for the 1961 Berlin crisis—the first to occur after Kennedy's adoption of 'flexible response'—specified that, should Moscow manage to 'encroach upon our vital interests', then three possible scenarios could ensue: 'A. Selective nuclear attacks for the primary purpose of demonstrating the will to use nuclear weapons. B. Limited tactical advantage . . . C. General Nuclear War.'[21] This was what was meant by flexibility.

The notion of limited nuclear war, confined to Europe, had particular

8

appeal to the Americans in the early 1960s because the Russians could by then reach the United States with long-range nuclear missiles. European officials, on the other hand, saw such a war as a stage towards a full nuclear exchange—and therefore as a guarantee that the Americans would involve themselves in any European conflict.[22] Be that as it may, the fact that US territory was now vulnerable to military attack by a major power for the first time since the eighteenth century was a constant source of anxiety to the US military in the 1960s and 1970s, and become a major refrain of the New Right's campaigns of the late 1970s. There was talk of developing a 'first strike capability'—to knock out Soviet missiles on their launching pads—and fresh attention was paid to ways of limiting war, either geographically or to particular types of weapon.[23] The Star Wars project—to be discussed later—was the main fruit of such strategic thinking.

A Soviet Threat?

From the historical evidence now available, very few Western leaders appear to have believed in 1949 that the USSR posed a military threat to the West. John Foster Dulles, later to become US Secretary of State, expressed himself quite clearly: 'I do not know of any responsible high official, military or civilian . . . in this government or any other government who believes that the Soviet now plans conquest by open military aggression.'[24] Nor did the CIA suggest at that time, in its various submissions to the Administration, that such a threat had been perceived by NATO intelligence. Finally, the British politician with the most ministerial experience of NATO, Denis Healey, has recently stated: 'There has been no time since the Second World War when Western intelligence believed the Russians had in their plans an all-out attack on Europe.'[25]

What, then, is left of the famous 'Soviet threat', which has always been the mainstay of Cold War politics and ideologies? Everything indicates that it was a conscious, and unscrupulous, invention of Western politicians seeking to shore up the post-war Atlantic order and to win the argument against alternative policy options. In the United States, the 'threat' was first used to swing congressional opinion at a time when the Administration was intent on breaking from long traditions in foreign policy—such as a reluctance to sign military treaties in peacetime, or to deploy troops outside the Americas. In Britain, Winston Churchill's image of an 'Iron Curtain' largely served to persuade the US Administration to bail out Britain's ailing economy with a huge loan. It would be easy to identify similar reasons why

Italian and German Christian Democrats, Spanish and Portuguese fascists, or the right wing of European social democracy, added their distinctive voices to the anti-Communist chorus of the late 1940s and 1950s.

We now know the true military balance that prevailed as the Cold War gathered momentum. By 1949 the Western media were talking of 175 Soviet divisions facing a mere 15 at the disposal of the West. But if we subtract all troops who would not have participated in battle, the actual situation was one of balance: Western Europe had a total of some 850,000 combat troops, while the Russians had fractionally less in their westward-facing divisions.[26] In the thirty-seven years of NATO's existence, the Soviet Union and its allies have never had a meaningful superiority in terms of troop levels.[27] It is true that Moscow used to threaten Western Europe with invasion, but it always did so as a retaliatory posture, in a period when the USSR was extremely vulnerable to a nuclear first strike.[28] Once the Soviet leadership had acquired the means to fire long-range missiles at the United States, it dropped all hints of launching an attack on Western Europe.

A serious study of the post-war world leads one to the conclusion that Europe is threatened with destruction (along with other parts of the world) not because of any Soviet intent, but because of the confrontation between the two blocs. Apart from those whose political imagery is derived from adolescent 'evil empire' films, no one has ever explained what the Soviet Union might hope to gain from an attack on Western Europe. The countries that *do* face Soviet military pressure, especially in Eastern Europe, also suffer as a direct result of the bloc antagonism between NATO and the Warsaw Pact. The final tightening of Moscow's control in Eastern Germany, Czechoslovakia and Hungary started in response to the development of a powerful anti-Communist bloc in the West, and the Soviet Union has justified subsequent military interventions, in East Germany, Hungary and Czechoslovakia, as being within the unwritten ground rules of the bi-polar system.

The Labour Party, in its most recent discussions on military policy, recognizes the dangers of East-West confrontation and sets as its long-term goal the dissolution of the blocs. But it will only be able to pursue the goal effectively if it tackles the task of dismantling the official mythology of the Russian menace that has sustained the Cold War for 40 years, and offers a more persuasive and realistic assessment of the dangers to world peace today.

NATO and British Politics

In 1951, two years after Britain helped to form NATO, a Labour government which had enjoyed widespread popular support was replaced by a Tory government that would last thirteen years. One of Labour's last measures, taken under US prompting, had been drastically to increase arms spending, even at the risk of undermining its proudest achievement, the still youthful National Health Service. This was to be just one example of the various pressures—economic, political, commercial and diplomatic —through which the United States has influenced decision-making at the highest levels, even if Britain has been spared the CIA-backed military coups that have ravaged other NATO countries.[29]

NATO has also strengthened certain elements of the British political Establishment which might otherwise have been relegated to its margins. For two US historians, the special relationship with America, sanctified with NATO's creation, meant that: 'All sorts of domestically redundant British soldiers, experts and ideas found a shelter under the American imperial mantle. For a fading British military elite, the special relationship extended the imperial function for one more generation and postponed a little longer the final reckoning with history. To be sure, as time went on, Britain's imperial pleasures would become increasingly vicarious rather than direct. Inexorably, she would seem more and more an American tributary.'[30]

The continued power of the 'fading military elite' has ensured, with NATO's assistance, that an abnormally high proportion of national income has been thrown at a bottomless pit called 'defence'. The end of empire did not see a reduction in such waste. Instead, the Atlantic Alliance came up with ever new demands for military roles and equipment that consumed steadily increasing amounts of public money. The intelligence establishment, for its part, provides an excellent example both of an antiquated institution revived and perpetuated by NATO, and of a part of traditional Britain which the Americans have increasingly taken over. Once a vanguard for 'intelligence' work, the secret service could have been reduced to minuscule proportions as Britain's role in the world declined. Instead, the Soviet bogey provided a cover under which numerous employees could engage themselves with 'threat watching', while hundreds of others whiled away their time listening to phone calls made by trade unionists, peace or civil liberties activists, and others. According to one ex-employee, phone-tapping was only one part of an operation which also encompassed attendance

11

at meetings, opening of mail and other intrusions into people's private lives.[31]

The Americans dominate intelligence activity in a number of ways, but mainly through their sole access to the most sensitive information and their right, by agreement, to decide what their allies see. The United States makes it a priority to ensure that the image of a 'threat' is upheld. The intelligence establishment in Britain, whose jobs depend on the survival of this image, is not inclined to challenge it, and tends to be more than receptive to the line peddled by the Americans.

In recent years, the US has come to hold sway to such an extent in the intelligence field that a British Government banned a trade union (at the spy HQ at Cheltenham) virtually under US orders. The Prime Minister relied on US intelligence to fight her war in the South Atlantic, while British military intelligence, which helped set up the CIA in 1947, is now little more than one of its out-stations. US domination even penetrates into certain specialist areas where the Soviet Union is less of a rival than many capitalist countries. In the field of energy (oil, gas, etc.), for example, a British minister may be denied access to information by the Americans, and must get approval through top civil servants.

Another central element of the special relationship is the presence of US bases. Here again, the ambition to maintain a 'Great Power' posture, on the part of both Labour and Tory ministers, has required and fostered its apparent opposite: a degree of servility to the United States which is quite remarkable even by NATO standards, representing a constant menace to basic civil liberties and the security of the population. As long ago as 1948, the US Air Force commander in Britain noted with astonishment the senile trustfulness of John Bull's public authorities: 'Never before in history has one first-class power gone into another first-class power's country without any agreement. We were just told to come over and "We shall be pleased to have you." '[32]

Within the Foreign Office, it was hoped that membership of NATO would silence any opposition to America's military presence. According to one 1950 memorandum, 'The existence of the Atlantic Pact and the principle of mutual aid enable us to accept the presence of a foreign air force in our territory as part of a general allied plan and without *appearing* to be surrendering our independence to the United States as such.'[33] Opposition did indeed die down. Consequently, since the early 1950s, over 25,000 Americans have had free access to sizeable chunks of British land, and have established for themselves the right to instal all kinds of weaponry there, to

12

prepare major nuclear offensives or limited operations in the Soviet bloc, and always with the full protection of British bobbies or squaddies.

Under the Visiting Forces Act of 1952, which established the legal position of US forces based here, the Americans can escape British justice when they run over British citizens, hold them at gunpoint, riot in towns, or otherwise violate laws of this country—as indeed they have done on occasion.[34] Those who object to some of the hardware the Americans introduce to the bases do however face the laws of the land—usually new ones specifically concocted to deal with them. Where laws fail, a couple of thousand men in khaki may be used instead, as happened at the cruise base of Molesworth

In the event of a crisis or war, US military commanders could have quite sweeping powers in this country. According to an Emergency Powers Bill passed by the Tory Cabinet, zones around key points such as bases, bridges, ports or major roads would be declared Ground Defence Areas (GDAs). Within these, residents 'may be expelled or forced to move according to US or British defence requirements ... Houses will be demolished to give free-fire zones. "Subversive" protesters or others within GDA areas can be detained without charge or trial.'[35]

The Emergency Powers might be enforced in the event of a crisis in which US forces wished to reach Central Europe rapidly, via the UK, from the United States, or to intervene in the Persian Gulf. As things stand, the British Parliament would have no say in the matter, since American 'defence requirements' are quite sufficient as a justification and there is no stipulation about where American forces might be operating. Under Emergency Powers (No. 2) Bill, moreover, powers inside the GDAs would be 'extended to cover the entire country.... The Home Secretary's Detention (internment) orders are automatically extended. Strikes in major industries are outlawed.'

The Americans recently gave a clear display of their disdainful attitude to the rights of allies, after US fighters unashamedly carried out a mid-air hijack of an Egyptian aircraft in October 1985. The plane was forced to land in Sicily, where there are US and Italian NATO bases. When Italian troops surrounded the unexpected visitor on landing, they suddenly found themselves facing the pointed rifles of their US friends and allies. A frantic telephone conversation took place between the Italian Prime Minister, Craxi, and President Reagan while their respective NATO troops tensely awaited orders. Reagan failed to persuade Craxi, despite enormous pressure, to hand over the Palestinians—who, after all, had hijacked an

Italian ship. Then the Americans made desperate efforts to harass the Italian soldiers conveying the hijackers to Rome, and to prevent the Italian government from releasing one Palestinian who had not been involved in the incident but whom the White House sought to implicate.

A still more recent episode, the use of bases in Britain for the Rambo-style attack on Libya, demonstrated the extent to which the Reagan Administration regards NATO as a matter of convenience for its own political and military goals, regardless of the letter of the Atlantic Treaty. The bases are supposed to be here because of NATO and the 'Soviet threat', as are the F1-11s fighters, the tanker-planes and the US back-up personnel in Britain. Yet in April 1986 we saw NATO planes leaving NATO bases from a NATO country to bomb undefended civilians and military installations in a non-NATO country with no formal military connection to the Soviet Union. Contrary to the misinformation spread at the time, there was not even a military reason for the use of distant bases in Britain: the authoritative *Jane's Fighting Ships* has shown that it was a purely political decision. Yet Parliament, for its part, had no more say over the use of the bases than had the Tory Cabinet.

The scant regard for the effect of US military operations in Britain for the safety of the British people is not a new phenomenon. On at least four occasions, US nuclear forces on British soil have been placed on a higher level of alert (ie, standby) in order to frighten Moscow or to prepare for nuclear war against the Russians. On the first two such occasions, the US military was considering the use of nuclear weapons in the Third World and wished to keep Moscow out of the way (Vietnam in 1954, Lebanon in 1958). The third occasion, when the world came closer than ever to a full-scale confrontation, was the Cuba crisis of 1962. The fourth was the Middle East conflict of 1973.[36]

British military leaders generally claim that they have been consulted over the use of British bases during these alerts—the least one might expect when, after all, the whole British Isles and much of the world was being put at risk. Yet, 'consultation' has amounted to little more than belated messages to military officials after decisions had been taken by the US military to proceed to higher states of alert.[37] The British top brass had no actual say in the matter, and the British people are still unaware for the most part of what took place.

There are a number of other ways in which NATO membership affects British politics and British society. The impact of high military spending on the economy—exacerbated by NATO agreements for real growth in arms

14

spending at times when welfare spending and capital investment are being held back—is one obvious example. The nuclear nexus, with weapons, energy and waste all bound up in a sorry mess of disinformation and official lies, is another. But such issues will not be dealt with here, except insofar as they have a direct bearing on the critique of present Labour policy outlined below.

Britain's Strategic Role

NATO, as we have seen, has four main functions: to support US plans for a nuclear conflict with the Soviet Union; to prepare for a conventional war with the Warsaw Pact; to back up America's role as global policeman; and to marginalize or suppress radical political forces in Western Europe. In all these respects, though less so in the last, Britain performs a number of important tasks.

1. Britain maintains some 55,000 troops and a large part of its air force on the NATO front in West Germany. It also has plans to transfer more than 100,000 reinforcements to the Federal Republic in the event of war—a scenario that is regularly rehearsed in major exercises. This whole military commitment was originally made to satisfy French demands in the 1950s that West German rearmament should not be allowed to threaten France.[38] It is now symbolic of a *political* resolve to take joint action within a NATO framework: the Alliance would not suffer militarily if five per cent of its troops in West Germany (Britain's effective contribution) were to be removed, although it is possible that the Belgians and Dutch would then follow suit.[39] A number of military critics, particularly in the Navy, have actually argued that the British deployment is part of a World War Two scenario which, hinging on the concept of land war, has little to do with present-day realities.[40]

2. Britain provides the greater part of NATO's Eastern Atlantic Fleet, whose principal function would be to protect US forces shipped to Europe in a war. In peacetime it generally patrols the sea-lanes, although it has been estimated that over a quarter of Britain's NATO frigates are currently in the South Atlantic for Falklands tasks.[41] Critics have argued that this too is based on a World War Two conception. For if there was a major war, we would all be dead before US ships could reach Europe. Missile-firing submarines, equipped with laser technologies, would anyway destroy a surface fleet in the first exchanges of a general war.[42]

3. Britain acts as an 'unsinkable aircraft carrier' for US nuclear forces

targeted on the Soviet Union—both F1-11s bombers based in this country, and B-52s that would need a stop-off point on their way to the USSR. Cruise missiles also require a European platform, although most of them could just as easily be launched from the sea. On the other hand, intercontinental missiles have rendered Britain's 'aircraft-carrier' role less vital, and many US bases would now be closed if they did not also serve other purposes.

4. Britain plays a role in NATO's early-warning system, but this is largely confined to detection of an air attack on these islands themselves—an unlikely eventuality. More important are the British facilities for tracking the movement of Soviet submarines through the Atlantic gap between the British Isles and Iceland.[43] Strictly speaking, Britain provides this service not to NATO but directly to the Americans, who pride themselves on their ability to locate any Soviet submarine anywhere in the world. Another US facility in Britain, Fylingdales, is linked to the US-controlled Ballistic Missile Early Warning System. With new equipment presently being installed, Fylingdales is likely to have a place in the Star Wars programme, and any possibility of its termination would be greeted with considerable anxiety in Washington.

5. Britain's submarine-based nuclear missiles, the main part of its nuclear force, are targeted in Omaha, Nebraska, with the participation of British officials and 'in accordance with Alliance policy and strategic concepts under plans made by SACEUR (the Supreme Commander of NATO)'. Polaris is thought to be targeted solely on Moscow—which is also 'covered' by US strategic forces and by Pershing II missiles based in West Germany.[44] It cannot be said, then, that the loss of Polaris would cause *military* problems for NATO, although, as we shall see, it would arouse a great deal of political concern.

6. Britain has a limited capacity to deploy naval forces or small mobile units outside the NATO area—for example, in the Persian Gulf.[45] These hardly amount to a significant back-up for US intervention, but Washington is keen to avoid isolation in such circumstances by enlisting the token support of one or more European allies. Other roles for Britain include: air force participation in any attack on the Warsaw Pact; anti-submarine warfare; sabotage activities; intelligence work inside the Soviet bloc and elsewhere; the defence of Britain's national territory and (together with US troops) of American bases located here; and specific assignments in the war game against Soviet positions in the Kola Peninsula.

In conclusion, Britain's own forces play a substantial role in the functioning of the Alliance. Although NATO would not automatically collapse if Britain were to leave, the key American presence in Europe would have to undergo major restructuring and reorientation—quite apart from the deep political concern that would be stirred by such a move.

Star Wars and Tension in NATO

When President Reagan unleashed Star Wars on the world in an extraordinary speech in March 1983, he had probably not given a moment's thought to its impact on the Atlantic Alliance. And yet, in some ways this bizarre but not impossible dream—to protect the territory of the United States from enemy missiles—could have more influence on intra-Alliance developments than any other single episode in NATO's history. Crises are not new to NATO. Indeed the Alliance has only just come through one of its more torrid periods as a consequence of its decision to deploy Cruise and Pershing II missiles in Western Europe. But the tensions thrown up by the Star Wars programme have highlighted divisions within the military, scientific, political and business establishments whose unity has sustained NATO all these years.

The Strategic Defence Initiative (SDI) threatens to undermine one of the underlying concepts of the Alliance, nuclear deterrence. For years NATO propaganda insisted that since nuclear weapons can always inflict unacceptable damage on an adversary, their potential use plays a unique role in deterring aggression and maintaining peace. There were always major problems with this argument, and the peace movement has laboured long and hard to expose them. But precisely because it appeared to make a general war unthinkable on both sides, deterrence had little attraction as an operational concept for Pentagon strategists. Then, at one stroke, Reagan appeared to offer a way out in the form of a shield against the devastating effects of nuclear retaliation. If the programme were ever to be—even partially—realized,[46] it would considerably increase Washington's room for manoeuvre in any East-West conflict, conferring an overwhelming superiority if only for the few years that its monopoly might last. Who would care to predict how that superiority might be used in the hands of Reagan or his successors?

Undoubtedly the Alliance can survive this latest blow. But the division that has now arisen between social democrats and liberal-conservatives—who align with the Russians in trying to save deterrence—and right-wing conservatives and fellow-travellers who dream of 'victory' is a real one. It is

17

spreading far into the ranks of the military as well as the political community on both sides of the Atlantic, and it will seriously impair top-level unity against any renewed outburst of popular opposition to NATO nuclear policies.

A short time ago, there was a flurry of articles in the press about moves to strengthen Western Europe's position in NATO in relation to the United States. The Western European Union—a moribund defence alliance—was rejuvenated; European arms cooperation became more extensive; an agenda was being set for European high-tech cooperation through the French-inspired Eureka programme; and the EEC was to start taking on greater responsibilities for foreign and defence policy. Star Wars has taken the heart out of all this. It has caused friction between France and West Germany, the two powers at the centre of the new moves; it has shown up the WEU to be utterly ineffectual; and it has spawned a host of US-European arms deals that outweigh the all-European contracts in value and volume, particularly so far as the British, West German and Italian governments are concerned. But the more independent-minded European leaders have grown distinctly cool, and Greece and Denmark have made it clear that they want nothing to do with the programme. While Star Wars has revealed official America to be more dominant in NATO than before, and also more manic and unaccountable, the European Establishment is increasingly riven with illusions that run through countries and parties as well as between nation-states.

A further NATO legend has it that the United States would always answer a West European call for military assistance in a crisis. When confidence in such aid is high, America is seen to be 'coupled' to Europe; when confidence is low, it is said to be 'decoupled'. Thus the SDI, which sends a strong message that America is attending to its own defence and leaving Europe to fend for itself, has ploughed deep furrows of anxiety across the brows of European Atlanticists. One response has been the ramshackle 'European Defence Initiative' (EDI)—a scheme which, because of the much shorter flight-time of incoming Soviet missiles, appears even less credible than America's fantastic Star Wars programme, although it might enjoy a brief life as a source of income for the arms industry and as a public relations exercise to mollify European opinion. Polls currently indicate that 57 per cent of the British population is 'not confident' that the United States would involve itself in the 'defence of Europe' in any eventuality.[17] Many would probably prefer that it didn't anyway, given that the 'crisis' might have been concocted in Washington. But for Europe's Atlanticist Establishment, something more serious than the EDI will be required to maintain its confidence in the direction of NATO strategy.

America and Europe's Future

In 1983 a NATO official expressed profound unease about the future of his employer: 'During the last two years, transatlantic tension between the United States and Europe has increased to the extent that many observers now question whether the United States and Europe continue to share the same interests and objectives. Indeed, many predict that the current differences represent the first stage of a change that is historically inevitable – the disengagement of the United States from Europe and a major transformation in the structure of Western security'.[48] The author was referring not merely to the Euromissiles furore but also to conflicts concerning protectionism on both sides of the Atlantic, US bans on high-tech exports to the Soviet bloc, European involvement in a major Soviet gas pipeline, US policy in Central America, and Western responses to the Soviet invasion of Afghanistan and the declaration of Martial Law in Poland. In most of these cases, mainland European leaders continued their earlier commitment to coexistence, trade and negotiations with the USSR. It is true that there were significant differences between Paris and Bonn, for example, over attitudes to the Soviet bloc. But essentially it was the policy of the United States that took a sharply different course at the turn of the seventies, with a desire to confront the Soviet Union head-on, to force down EEC barriers to US trade, to limit Western Europe's competitiveness in high technology, to loosen the Soviet grip on Eastern Europe, and so on.

This new policy was not a maverick departure from the norm, but reflected deep-seated shifts within the United States itself that will also shape any post-Reagan administration. The most important of these is the extremely rapid growth of the economies of America's South and West. Until the 1970s the states on the East Coast and the Great Lakes always produced the greatest part of America's national product and threw up most of its business and political leaders as natural Atlanticists. Today, the South and West hold more than half the US population and account for more than half of its total output. Sunbelt politicians and businessmen play an ever more prominent role in Washington, and their interests are spread widely in the Pacific, Latin America and the Middle East. Although they have by no means lost sight of Europe, they see little sense in committing half of the US military budget to the NATO area—where rich allies are quite capable of taking over much of the routine, 'low-tech' military burden. Instead, they consider the main priorities to be the Rapid Deployment Force, the SDI and other grand schemes that will strengthen the United States as a global power, capable of unilaterally policing any part of the world in which it has strategic or commercial interests.[49]

Much of the tension in NATO in the early 1980s resulted from pressure on the Europeans to comply with the demands of America's 'globalists'. Faced with the choice between concessions to the US on East-West relations or economic policy and a reduction in America's contribution to NATO, the European Establishment always moved just far enough to pacify the globalists. The victory over the peace movement—a victory not only for the White House but, in the end, also for the European Right—won over many doubters in the United States who had considered that a failure to instal Cruise and Pershing would serve to confirm Europe's pusillanimity. Now, however, the 'astronomic' cost of the SDI programme has placed great strain on the US military budget, reviving calls for partial US troop withdrawals from Europe and demands for Europe to 'pay its way' in NATO.

For all these reasons, it is somewhat naive for politicians in Western Europe to put their faith in a halcyon post-Reagan era, when reasonableness will return to Washington and NATO will be pulled back into shape. Like it or not, Europe will have to face up to a sea-change that no likely US administration will have the power or the inclination to reverse. When Henry Kissinger, an ardent Atlanticist, demanded in March 1984 that Europeans should assume more of the NATO burden on pain of US withdrawal, he was voicing a deep fear that forces beyond his control might undo all his work to strengthen NATO. This is not just another crisis for the Alliance, he wrote: 'the present controversies in NATO are both unprecedented and unsettling.'[50] The choice for Europeans is therefore increasingly limited: either to fall in with US global policies, starving our welfare states to feed their insatiable military machine; or to undertake a drastic change in course of our own. This will be the theme of Part Two.

20

Part Two:
Labour and NATO

Labour's Military Policies

As we have seen, the Labour Party was a staunch supporter of NATO from the beginning: it rarely questioned the ruling consensus on nuclear matters, and any attempts to do so were quickly quelled. It is therefore very much to be welcomed that, in the past few years, Labour has joined the growing number of opposition parties in Western Europe that are breaking from aspects of NATO orthodoxy.

The present Labour Party position, as expressed in its recent document *Defence and Security for Britain* and in various speeches and interviews from leading spokespeople, is as follows:

(a) Cruise missiles will be removed from British soil.

(b) The Trident submarine programme will be cancelled.

(c) Other British nuclear weapons will be phased out over time, ideally after discussions with the Russians to secure reductions by both parties.

(d) The Americans will be asked to remove four major nuclear bases (Greenham, Molesworth, Upper Heyford and Holy Loch)—the other 130 US bases and facilities being allowed to stay if the Americans agree to the deal.

(e) Britain will remain committed to NATO. (The recent defence document, approved by the 1984 Party conference, 'is the firmest re-statement of Labour's commitment to NATO for decades'.[51])

(f) Labour will seek to move towards a situation where the mutual dissolution of NATO and the Warsaw Pact becomes possible.

(g) Spending on non-nuclear weapons will remain high—indeed increase to take up the shock from cancellation of nuclear arms programmes.

(h) Labour will seek to strengthen the European bloc within NATO and encourage, for example, joint Western European exercises.

(i) British participation in Star Wars will not be encouraged, but it remains unclear whether the Party will vigorously oppose all aspects of Star Wars, including the European dimension.

21

The first question that immediately poses itself in relation to these proposals is whether they are consistent with Labour's declared support for unilateral nuclear disarmament and a progressive military policy in general. The plans covered in (a), (b) and (c) do point in this direction, although some leading figures in the Party have made no secret of their opposition to full unilateral nuclear disarmament unless it involves a Soviet quid pro quo.

More important, the policy on US bases is disingenuous insofar as it seeks to give the impression that only the most obvious sites for nuclear weapons are part of the US nuclear capability in this country. According to detailed investigative work by Duncan Campbell and others, the 135 or so US bases and facilities in Britain include the following:

—Main operation bases for various tactical fighter, reconnaissance and missile wings of the US Air Force, most of which have considerable nuclear capabilities. These wings would be used in a war in either Europe or the Middle East, regardless of Britain's involvement in that war.

—Stand-by operating bases, mainly for the use of US Air Force wings in a crisis or war, especially in the Middle East. These too would have considerable nuclear capabilities.

—'Collocated operating bases', as they are called, which are bases adapted for the use of US forces deployed to the European or Middle East 'theatres' in a crisis or war. These forces would also have nuclear weapons.

—Control centres for US cruise missiles based in and around Britain (this at High Wycombe); for US naval forces, including nuclear submarines, to the north and east of Scotland; for USAF operations (including nuclear); and for various types of intelligence activity.

—The Fylingdales station in North Yorkshire, which would help to guide America's strategic nuclear arsenal and eventually Star Wars weapons.

—Various intelligence establishments with a range of functions, including spying on various groups, among them trade unions, held to be subversive or anti-Establishment.

—Ammunition dumps, including storage dumps for nuclear weapons.

—Communication facilities for US nuclear and other forces.

—Transportation facilities and other supply and support facilities.[52]

To remove four well-known US bases and leave the rest in place will scarcely bring us nearer to a non-nuclear Britain. If the concern is the role of Britain as a front-line state in US war plans, or as a target in any major war, then these will be unaffected; if the concern is Britain's implication in any US war in the Middle East, then Labour's policy is not the answer; if the concern is American violations of British sovereignty, or US interference in Britain's domestic politics, then once again there will be no change.

The limitations of Labour's policy on bases were made glaringly apparent by the US operation against Libya in April 1986. F1-11s were given license to fly from various bases, among them 'nuclear' Upper Heyford and 'non-nuclear' Lakenheath. Yet there was no guarantee that the F1-11s would not be carrying nuclear wapons, and no possibility of stopping them if they had been. Those responsible for giving the US a green light to use the bases, among them Thatcher and Howe, have said that it was not possible to refuse permission without threatening the alliance with America. Is the alliance not also sacrosanct for Labour? There is nothing in its present policy to suggest that a Labour government would have stopped such an operation, or that it would have been any more aware of what weapons were on board.

Labour's support in the opinion polls rose in the immediate aftermath of the Libya attack to the highest point since before the Falklands War (39-43 per cent). The fact that Labour is the only party to advocate the closure of any bases was undoubtedly a factor in this, not least because support for the closure of US bases in Britain was running considerably higher than support for Labour in the period of the attack. The evidence of numerous polls is that few people distinguish between nuclear and non-nuclear bases, and by making a distinction, Labour is pleasing no one but the Americans.[53]

A Non-Nuclear NATO?

Similar difficulties arise with Labour's declared commitment to remain a member of NATO, while seeking to move it away from a policy of *first use* and *early use* of nuclear weapons. Somehow this fails to take account of the hard reality that the United States has dominated the Atlantic Alliance from the outset, as its principal military and economic power. All NATO's strategic nuclear weapons are American, and the US Establishment decides on how to expand, modernize or otherwise develop them. Most of NATO's short and medium-range nuclear weapons are American, or are controlled by NATO countries with the US President having the final say over use. It is

23

the US President who would decide, together with his chief advisers, when to launch a nuclear war—although there is always the possibility of some consultation with NATO allies.

NATO is nothing if not nuclear: it was born as an alliance committed to the use of nuclear weapons, and it will die as one. Shorn of its nuclear strategy it would be shorn of American power, and would no longer be NATO but a West European alliance.

If Britain opts to abandon its own nuclear weapons *within* NATO, it is opting to rely on America's nuclear weapons in a crisis. This is still a nuclear option, and still a suicide option. Denzil Davies, Labour spokesperson on defence matters, said as much in an interview with *END Journal* in mid-1985: If war were declared, 'we would accept NATO strategy at that point.... The Party is committed to staying in NATO. It has never said that if NATO doesn't change strategy it is going to withdraw Britain from NATO.... We believe being part of NATO is the best possible defence for Britain.'

This remarkable statement would suggest that current Labour leaders have only a rhetorical commitment to 'breaking up the military blocs', and that it has no intention of questioning its commitment to NATO if and when the Alliance fails to change its nuclear stategy under Labour pressure. It also leaves Labour wide open to Tory election tactics. According to the *Times* (28 October 1985), Tory advisers have it in mind to challenge Labour to say where the ousted Americans should go to. 'Should they resite their nuclear weapons on the Continent, or should they take them home?' they will ask. 'If Labour answers that they should go to the Continent it will be acknowledging that Britain wants American protection but it is not prepared to offer the facilities to provide it. If Labour says the weapons should be taken home it will be saying that it is prepared to see Britain undefended by nuclear weapons.' The only coherent answer to the question is that Labour seeks to remove the weapons and the bases as part of a general international policy whereby any potential threats to Britain will be effectively dealt with by non-nuclear (and preferably non-military) means, and whereby the reliance on America's nuclear 'protection' will be replaced by a commitment to work with a new range of allies to break down the military blocs and bring an end to nuclear confrontation. Such a path is not consistent with staying in the Atlantic Alliance.

24

Are Labour's Proposals Coherent?

At the Labour Party Conference in 1983, Denis Healey asserted that there was a fundamental inconsistency between staying in NATO and unilaterally abandoning nuclear weapons. Healey himself has since changed his tone on the matter, but it is commonly felt, on both the left and right of the Party, that what he said holds true. Of course NATO is not a monolith, and different elements within it would react in different ways to various aspects of Labour's military policies. It is therefore necessary to be clear that we are essentially talking about the likely response of the US Establishment, as manifested through the ruling bodies of NATO and other institutions. Let us consider Labour's policy commitments in turn.

(a) Cruise missiles. In his recent Fabian essay *Labour and a World Society*, Denis Healey argued that since Cruise missiles 'serve no military purpose' and 'undermine public support for the Alliance', there would be no problem, from NATO's point of view, if they were removed from Britain. There is some truth in this. The US Establishment is divided between those who have always seen the Cruise deployment as irrelevant and not worth defending, and those who consider the missiles to be a vital symbol of 'NATO cohesion'.[54] For its part, the NATO European Establishment is divided between those who believe that the Alliance gained more than it lost from deployment and those who believe the opposite.

In such a context, a policy of returning Cruise to sender could conceivably escape NATO's wrath—but only if it was pursued as an isolated element of an essentially pro-nuclear policy. If Labour is to remain faithful to its own advocacy of non-nuclear defence, it can therefore expect to meet with great resistance inside NATO to the removal of Cruise missiles from Britain. At present the Labour leadership does not seem prepared to face up to the likely consequences that it would incur in government.

(b) Trident. The United States has never fully come to terms with Britain's own nuclear capability, at times withholding 'secrets' to slow it down and ultimately tolerating it only because of benefits derived from bases in Britain or overseas, or from the provision of plutonium. This schizophrenic approach has generally combined public support for Britain's right to have nuclear weapons with private criticism of its independent nuclear policy. The US attitude to the Trident programme appears at one level to be more unambiguously positive. NATO's Nuclear Planning Group, dominated by US officials, has declared Trident to be a matter of 'fundamental importance' to the Alliance as a whole, while Caspar Weinberger, US Secretary of

Defense, has declared that 'the United States attaches great importance to the maintenance by the United Kingdom government of an independent nuclear deterrent'. Thus Britain buys at great cost a high-tech system whose accuracy requires full assistance from US satellites and which cannot be serviced without US aid. In return, America sings its praises and calls for more of the same. In reality, things are not so simple. The same Caspar Weinberger has since become an ardent champion of Star Wars which, if reciprocated on the Soviet side, would rapidly make Trident's long-range missiles obsolete.[55]

Trident had confused and divided the British military Establishment even before Star Wars. For it represents a drastic escalation in Britain's nuclear armoury, taking the number of strategic warheads to over a thousand and threatening to undermine future spending on conventional military forces, especially new ships. It is not even clear that it was meant to worry the Soviet Union and 'enhance deterrence'. John Nott, the defence minister responsible for the decision, explained to the House of Commons on 11 March 1982 that since NATO may not last for ever, 'in the last resort Great Britain must be responsible for its own defence'; and that the Cabinet was not prepared to consider a course of action which would leave 'the French, our immediate neighbour, as the only European nuclear power'. These statements, echoing private comments by other Tory ministers,[56] suggest a greater disquiet about the old enemy across the Channel than about the Russians. It is little wonder that over seventy per cent of the population opposes Trident.

Again, Labour appears well placed to divide the potential opposition, both within NATO and at home, to one of its anti-nuclear policies. Few feathers would be ruffled in Brussels and deep dismay would surface only in certain sections of the Ministry of Defence. The Americans, for their part, would surely do no more than growl at the loss of a lucrative military contract. Why, then, have Labour spokesmen repeatedly found it necessary to *compensate* for cancellation of the Trident order, as if the Party feared a tidal wave of opposition to its policy from within the Western Alliance? To switch the saved money into job creation and welfare spending, following years of Tory neglect, would surely appeal far more to prospective Labour voters. It would also benefit the British economy as a whole, which has suffered from decades of high military spending by Labour and Tory governments alike.

(c) Polaris. Is the Labour Party going to pursue only the less controversial anti-nuclear policies open to it, thereby diluting its non-nuclear commitment

and dividing the peace movement? Or will it press ahead with policies that would take Britain forward to full unilateral nuclear disarmament, even at the price of entering into conflict with the NATO Alliance? In the debate about Polaris, we can see the main lines of the dilemma emerge with particular clarity.

Polaris missile-carrying submarines, in Britain's possession for over two decades now, differ markedly from Trident in their volume of firepower, their military effectiveness and their level of technological sophistication. What interests us here, however, is their different political implications at the present point in time. To scrap Trident would not *necessarily* be a unilateralist measure—as shown by the policy of the SDP to replace it with sea-launched cruise missiles. The decommissioning of Polaris, on the other hand, has become a benchmark for unilateral nuclear disarmament, and its retention would do most to appease opinion in NATO and to prevent Labour's non-nuclear policies from inspiring similar moves elsewhere in the world. It is therefore not surprising to find the Labour leadership attempting to weaken precisely the unilateralist element of an anti-Polaris policy. Thus Denis Healey writes in his Fabian pamphlet that Neil Kinnock's deal with Moscow, whereby the Soviet Union will dismantle one Soviet missile for every British missile removed, undermines the unilateralist principle: 'What was once a unilateral commitment,' he writes, 'has become a *bilateral* one.' More recently, the Shadow Foreign Secretary has suggested that this deal is now out of date. 'Chernenko,' he argues 'was talking about reducing the number of SS-20s by the number of Polaris missiles. Now the Russians are saying they'll get rid of the SS-20s entirely if the Americans get rid of Cruise and Pershing.... Do we unilaterally get rid of Polaris whatever happens, or do we accept the Soviet proposal to negotiate about its future in the second stage of the arms negotiations? This will have to be resolved before the election.'[57] There is no doubt about the answer that Denis Healey would give. Regardless of conference resolutions, then, it would appear that the argument for unilateral nuclear disarmament has not yet been won in the Party.

(d) The US Bases. According to Denzil Davies, 'The closure of US nuclear bases would concern America (and possibly West Germany) more than the ending of Britain's role as a semi-independent nuclear power. But closure of nuclear bases would have been a decision of the British people.... NATO is a collection of democratic states and stands for democracy and respect for the democratic process' (*END Journal*, Summer 1985). Denis Healey, for his part, is confident that 'it should not be difficult to persuade the Americans

to withdraw their nuclear bases from Britain. It is doubtful whether they will need the submarine base at Holy Loch once the (American) Trident submarines are in service. And their F1-11 bombers are likely to be of little value by the time the next general election comes to Britain. If the United States regarded Britain as a valuable ally in NATO, we should be able to persuade it to withdraw its existing nuclear bases from Britain.'[58]

These two statements, reflecting rather different conceptions of NATO, are both based on shaky assumptions. The least tenable is undoubtedly Davies's idealization of the Alliance as a 'collection of democratic states'. There has been virtually no time in its history when all member-countries have enjoyed a free democratic system safe from outside interference. Portugal's fascist regime was a member of NATO until it fell in 1974, military dictatorships in Greece and Turkey have at various times had a full place in the Alliance, and Franco's Spain, though never actually a member, provided invaluable military services to the Americans. Moreover, NATO powers—above all, the United States—have been directly implicated in the overthrow of democratically elected governments within the Alliance, not to mention the appaling US record in sponsoring military coups in Latin America and elsewhere.[59]

Denis Healey is thus right to weigh the possibility of US attempts to sabotage a Labour decision to close four major nuclear bases. What is questionable is his suggestion that the reduced strategic value of these bases makes US interference less likely. The PASOK government in Greece has twice come to power on a platform of removing US bases. The intelligence role of some of these has been largely superseded by satellites; and the nuclear role of others is less relevant since the deployment of Cruise and Pershing. Even Greece's port facilities for the US Sixth Fleet can be replaced by a number of other countries. Yet the Americans have applied various forms of naked pressure—in particular, threats to withhold military and economic aid—in order to prevent a shutdown of their bases.

The reasons for this would seem obvious. Washington established its three thousand or more overseas bases in order to police the *pax Americana*, to threaten the USSR and to guard investments and strategic minerals. Withdrawal from any one base might encourage a widepread allergy on the part of host governments, with potentially disastrous results for American power. Even if some bases are less important than others, they all increase US options in a crisis or war. The US military, as it points out all too often, never knows which bases would be put out of action.

(e) Spending on Conventional Forces. For some time now Labour leaders

28

have been promising that spending on conventional forces will remain at similar levels and perhaps climb higher than under the present government. At first glance, this appears astonishing. The Thatcher Cabinet is one of the most militaristic since the war. It has been responsible for higher real increases in military spending than almost any government in NATO Europe since 1979. It has kept afloat ships which one of its own defence ministers dubbed 'floating gin-palaces' devoid of military value. And it is allocating 3 to 5 per cent of its military budget on holding Fortress Falklands. One might thus expect even a 'wet' Conservative government to bring down the level of military spending, at least far enough for the rest of the economy to begin to breathe again. Yet Labour seems oblivious of the overall consequences of its armaments programme.

On a broader view, this is somewhat less difficult to explain. Since the earliest days of NATO, a powerful nexus has consolidated itself in the major Western countries that acts as a constant push factor on the arms budget. In Britain the nexus includes the big companies involved in this sector, the scientists, strategists and military top brass, the relevant civil servants in the Treasury and the Ministry of Defence, and last but not least the politicians. As the empire withered in post-war Britain, there was always an array of 'NATO tasks' to fill the gap, and to justify a new round of increases. Today, with some 95 per cent of the military budget earmarked for such tasks, Britain spends more of its national income on the military than in the late nineteenth and early twentieth centuries, when it was policing a quarter of the globe and a sizeable chunk of the world's population. It is inconceivable that the militarist nexus at the heart of the Establishment could have built its enormous power without the help of NATO. By committing itself to continued membership, the Labour Party is ensuring that this power remains intact.

It would appear from *Defence and Security for Britain* and subsequent statements that Labour's policy on conventional arms spending is designed to help transform NATO, from within, into a non-nuclear alliance. For example, the Rhine Army or the Eastern Atlantic Fleet could be made stronger but non-nuclear and used as a lever to denuclearize all NATO forces in West Germany and the Eastern Atlantic respectively. The most likely effect of such a policy is that large sums would be expended on state-of-the-art conventional weaponry, only for subsequent Tory or SDP ministers to add back on the nuclear arsenal. Perhaps the most disturbing aspect, however, is that it is not a policy for peace but a different way of planning wars. Instead of actively working to break down tension on the Central Front, and to erode the whole political-ideological and military edifice of the 'Iron Curtain', Labour would be taking over nearly all the Cold War assumptions of its predecessors.

A Fluid Public Opinion

After this review of the contradictions of Labour's present policy, we must now consider an alternative which could take us further down the road to peace, and also win over a large part of the electorate. Those who advocate continued British membership of NATO usually put forward four arguments: that NATO deters the threat from the East; that it is an alliance of our friends in the world; that it costs less than a self-reliant national defence system; and that it assures American protection in a major war.

These arguments may carry much weight on the Right of British politics, but no single one could command a majority in the Labour Party or the trade union movement. There, the trump card that is advanced in internal discussions, though rarely before the general public, is that withdrawal would have adverse *electoral* implications for Labour. Opinion polls, showing a range of 6 to 14 per cent for withdrawal and around 80 per cent for continued membership, seem to confirm this judgement. However, the evidence of opinion polls always has to be handled with circumspection, particularly as respondents are generally reluctant to express a view that is negative in form. Thus, a private poll conducted in autumn 1985 produced a figure of 30 per cent in favour of Britain being 'neutral between East and West'—which would inevitably imply a breaking of the NATO link.'[61] It would be interesting to hear the result of a survey which asked whether people would approve of leaving NATO as part of a process of detente leading to the dissolution of blocs and the formation of a united Europe.

In early 1982 Gallup presented the question: 'Which one of the statements listed comes closest to your own view on how Britain should provide for its security in the 1980s?' The responses are extremely interesting:

—Continue in the NATO alliance, with Western Europe, the US and Canada: 37%
—Establish within NATO a unified West European defence force under European command, but allied to the US 20%
—Withdraw our military forces from NATO but otherwise remain in NATO for such things as policy consultation 5%
—Establish an independent West European defence force under European command but *not* allied to the US 10%
—Rely on our nation's defence forces without belonging to any military alliance 11%
—Reduce our emphasis on military defence and rely on greater accommodation with the USSR 5%
—Don't know 12%

Thus, only 57 per cent supported the military commitment to NATO, and 20 per cent of those would prefer an alliance less dominated by the United States—an option which, we have argued, is hardly open. On the other side, 26 per cent favoured an option involving withdrawal from NATO, with another 5 per cent wishing to opt out of military responsibilities to the Alliance.

The figures here are too soft for serious analysis. But together with the previous poll result, they do indicate a fluidity of opinion that undercuts the myth of 'solid support for NATO'. Further evidence was provided by a *Newsweek* poll in September 1985, which found minority support for the two main planks of NATO propaganda. Only 41 per cent considered the Soviet Union to be an expansionist power 'that threatens Western security', while 46 per cent saw it as 'mainly defensive in nature' and posing 'no threat to Western security'.

In another poll, in 1984, only 26 per cent of a sample of over two thousand believed that the Soviet Union 'posed a greater threat to world peace than America'; 11 per cent considered the United States to be the greater menace; and 54 per cent saw the two Superpowers as equivalent in this respect.[62] As the authors of this study point out, the figures are 'quite remarkable'. They run counter to what people are thought to believe in the West, and they bear no relation to the thrust of media information.

Of course, it is not our view that the Labour Party should base its policies on the results of opinion polls. Instead, it should place far greater emphasis on political principle, and on consistency between policies, drawing strength from the opportunity to change a volatile public's way of thinking through a concerted campaign that presents imaginative, progressive and radical policies. We could start by explaining what NATO is and how it works in practice—as the majority of the population appears to have no clear idea. The facts themselves will suggest at least five areas in which supporters of NATO are especially vulnerable.

(a) The United States is on the offensive within NATO. The new breed of American leaders, typified by Reagan and evidently here to stay, are predisposed to take decisions unilaterally and to bully rather than collaborate with Western Europe. As long as the Europeans remain in an alliance with the United States, they will be exposed to the full range of economic and political pressures that Washington can bring to bear upon governments that do not toe the line in military policy.

(b) Indicative of the present state of affairs is the new American plan for limited wars in Europe and the Third World. AirLand Battle—as it is called

—assigns a major role to Cruise missiles and Pershing II, in a full inter-linking of nuclear, chemical and conventional weapons designed to knock out the 'enemy' deep in its own territory almost before it has had time to move.[63] Contrary to the image of NATO as a purely defensive alliance, a first-strike capability is thus an essential component of its military policy.

(c) The Star Wars programme involves a huge military drive in a 'theatre' previously almost free of weapons. Launched by the United States alone, without conclusive evidence of similar Soviet moves, Star Wars was not presented for discussion within NATO or even, initially, within the US miliary establishment. It is an inherently destabilizing initiative, potentially posing a far greater threat to peace than the Euromissiles or the expansion of America's strategic arsenal set underway by the Reagan Administration. The Tory Cabinet's servile enthusiasm for the project casts a revealing light on Britin's 'special relationship' with the United States and on the disastrous road down which NATO is heading.

(d) The Euromissiles should not be forgotten, even as most eyes turn to the insane waste of human and economic resources involved in Star Wars. The decision by Washington and its European allies to impose Cruise and Pershing II, against majority opinion in most deployment countries, was perfect testimony to NATO's real purpose and undemocratic character. Labour should lose no opportunity to draw the appropriate conclusions, and to demonstrate the role of the Euromissiles in US/NATO war plans.

(e) NATO policies have already had a dire effect on basic liberties in Britain. The continued harassment of women and other peace activists; the rights given to US troops to attack and, if necessary, to shoot demonstrators inside Greenham; the denial to peace protesters of the elementary rights to travel freely in their own area at night or to use their telephone without interference by the state; the installation of a Wapping-style wall around Molesworth common land—these and other processes give the lie to NATO's self-declared mission of 'defending peace and security'.

The Basic Case against NATO

Against this sombre background, a basic case can now be made against NATO—óne which has already been taken up, in principle, by a large number of constituency Labour parties and several trade union leaders.[61] It should be carried deep into the labour movement where support is most vital.

1. NATO was supposedly established to deal with the possibility of a Soviet

attack upon Western Europe, and this has been the basis for all Western militarist rhetoric since the Cold War began. There is no factual ground for such an assumption, and while people continue to believe it they may never accept Labour's non-nuclear defence policy or its goal of disbanding NATO and the Warsaw Pact.

2. NATO membership has entailed a militarization of Britain without parallel in an era of peace between the major powers. The symptoms are a proliferation of bases, military installations and military manoeuvres; an economy distorted by military spending; and a position for the military in the Establishment far stronger than is appropriate for a freely operating parliamentary democracy.

3. NATO is dominated by the USA economically, politically and militarily. It is seen in Washington as a way of opposing socialism worldwide and maintaining American hegemony in Europe—just as her other military pacts, like ANZUS, do in other parts of the world.

4. NATO ministers have tended to remove military outlays from the normal public expenditure procedures, requiring them to expand at a fixed percentage at the expense of world development aid and domestic social programmes. US pressure has also secured British financing of the Star Wars project, which is militarily destabilizing and will drain technology towards the United States.

5. American bases and nuclear weapons in Britain, legitimized by NATO membership, are under sole US control. When the New Zealand government demanded to know whether visiting US warships were carrying nuclear weapons, it received curt advice to mind its own business. Its subsequent banning of such visits triggered an angry response from the United States, including threat of economic sanctions and its exclusion from ANZUS councils. This shows NATO to be deceiving us when it says that member states can take decisions quite freely.

6. NATO can contribute to the erosion of civil liberties, as has happened steadily in Britain for much of the post-war era. Civil defence planning within NATO is aimed more against domestic dissent than any external foe, as was shown by the Greek military coup of 1967. The deployment of NATO nuclear missiles at Greenham Common and Molesworth has already led the government to use military and police powers to crush civil liberties.

7. Despite the argument that acceptance of US bases, plus a nuclear force of its own, give Britain influence with the United States and a seat at top-level arms control talks, this country has been excluded from all superpower negotiations. In any case Britain, like the USA, has a consistent record of opposing disarmament.

33

8. The reality of the so-called special relationship is that Britain is a client state, dependent on US military technology and intelligence for the production and operation of its nuclear weapons. In return, the British government is expected to accept US missiles and to furnish Washington with all the intelligence it gathers through its own security services. As the 1986 attack on Libya showed, the extra-territoriality of the USAF includes the right to launch acts of aggression, outside the NATO area, from its bases in Britain.

9. NATO membership provides a cover for right-wing elements to take up safe and secure posts within the intelligence agencies. From this base, they are able to label domestic critics as 'subversive'; to spy on people committed to social change in Britain; to use hawkish assessments of the 'threat' to influence military spending in an upward direction; to protect their own activities, and those of related institutions, from public scrutiny; and to monitor international communications, whether personal or commercial.

10. NATO membership creates enemies and moulds Britain's foreign policy, barring any initiative that might reduce tension in Europe or offer radical solutions to serious problems in the Third World.

11. NATO would not defend Western Europe in a military conflict with the Warsaw Pact but ensure its rapid and near-total destruction. Plans for 'limited nuclear war', issuing from the US commanders of NATO, are a threat to the very survival of this continent.

12. NATO has facilitated the prosecution of thoroughly reactionary wars by member states: Indochina (1950 – 54) and Algeria (1955 – 62) in the case of France; Mozambique, Angola and Guinea-Bissau (1961 – 75) in the case of Portugal; Malaysia (1950 – 59) and the South Atlantic (1982) in the case of Britain; Korea (1950 – 53), Vietnam (1961 – 73) Lebanon (1958) and countless other interventions in the case of the United States.

13. Behind the rhetoric of deterrence, NATO acts as an effective guarantor of safe markets and high profits for the arms industries, and as a conduit for the diversion of valuable research and development from the civilian to the military sector.

14. NATO membership is wholly inconsistent with a policy designed to reduce tension and to bring peace to Europe and elsewhere. A policy of active non-alignment, on the other hand, would make it possible to eliminate Britain's relations of dependence and to establish foreign relations suited to world peace and security and the country's own long-term interests.

34

Towards a Campaign for Withdrawal

Perhaps the very first task in building a campaign for withdrawal from NATO is to convince the core of CLP and trade union activists that other directions are genuinely possible. 'There is no alternative'—as false a slogan in foreign policy as in internal politics—can acquire a deadening power unless it is consistently challenged by well researched and reasoned arguments, particularly as it refers, in the case of NATO, to structures that have been in place for two generations. As it happens, however, we need only look across the Channel to find a major European country that has significantly altered the American ground-plan for the West. It is now twenty years since General de Gaulle declared that NATO 'no longer corresponded to the prevailing world conditions', and although France has continued to participate in NATO councils and minor defence arrangements, its military forces have never again been integrated into the Atlantic command structure. Further to the north, Denmark and Norway provide examples of NATO countries which have refused to accept nuclear weapons on their territory. Of course, we are not sugesting that Labour should take any of these countries as its model: France retains, and is currently expanding, its independent nuclear *force de frappe*, as part of its lingering ambitions as a world power; Denmark and Norway have kept their armed forces at the disposal of the Alliance. Yet each, in its way, does present a striking contrast to the supine Atlanticism of successive British governments.

What we are proposing is to go a step further than these three NATO states: that is to say, full denuclearization of the national territory, plus withdrawal from NATO's military structures and refusal of bases or other facilities for the Pentagon's operations in Europe; but, in addition, withdrawal from all other NATO structures. Some may baulk at the latter and argue that Britain, like France, could still participate in the planning of NATO defence budgets, force goals etc., and in discussion of educational, scientific and related matters. However, the recent experience of Spain, where the government used non-integration into NATO's military command merely as a temporary device to see it through the referendum campaign, is a sobering pointer to the kind of pressure that would always be applied to Britain so long as it remained formally associated with the Alliance. Sweden, on the other hand, already shows that it is perfectly possible for a Western nation to opt out of the system of Western militarism, and to adopt a relatively progressive, independent foreign policy. But the recent murder of Olof Palme—according to its most plausible interpretation—also shows that there are forces in the West who will stop at nothing to silence discordant notes.

Britain's Labour leadership, while drawing inspiration from Olof Palme's courage, should be aware that there can be no stopping half-way, and that every ounce of determination and popular support would have to be mobilized to face the ruthless holy alliance that would fight any move to withdraw one of the major European countries from NATO. Lining up against it would be generals and admirals, big businessmen and bankers, media pundits and proprietors, American and West German leaders, and politicians from nearly every large political party.

The British Establishment is capable of mounting a powerful and sustained campaign, which would not necessarily abide by the Queensberry rules. The prospect of such opposition, and above all of direct US intervention, prompts many who are opposed to NATO to suggest either a policy of changing the Alliance from within, or one of moving step by step towards withdrawal. The first of these has been discussed and criticized earlier. The main problem with the second is that it is more likely to *assist* than to weaken the coalition of NATO diehards. Thus, whereas a declaration of intent to withdraw within one year—the minimum period under existing treaty obligations—would leave no room for doubt or ambiguity, a policy of gradual disengagement over a period of, say, five years would give the opposition far too much time to mount a counter-attack. It is also possible that the government would be replaced before the schedule had been fully implemented.

If the policy of withdrawal is based on a fundamental rejection of the principles and ideology behind the Atlantic Alliance, then there seems to be no valid reason for a middle-of-the-road alternative. Popular support will only be won and maintained so long as there is genuine excitement about the prospect of Britain's embarking on a new, non-aligned course in foreign policy. A reliance on stop – go, on fudge and nudge, is not the way to arouse enthusiasm for such a dramatic turn in the country's relationship with the world.

Labour and the Trade Unions

Tony Benn and Eric Heffer have already circulated a document to the Labour NEC and a number of groups and ward parties which has provided a useful focus for advancing the anti-NATO cause. It is hoped that, with the aid of this pamphlet, the basic case can win over the vast majority of constituency parties to support for a NATO-free Britain and a NATO-free Europe.[65] This will require its translation into a number of forms of media; the preparation of speakers' notes and meetings throughout the country; and a further development of arguments and concrete proposals for the realignment of Britain's foreign relations.

A central and immediate task will be to win over opinion within the trade union movement. Many leaders, for example, still fear the possible damage to Labour's electoral chances, or the risk that a hostile reaction to a motion on NATO would jeopardize hard-won positions in favour of unilateral nuclear disarmament. It will be necessary to develop arguments specifically geared to the interests of trade union members, in addition to those already outlined so far. In this process there are some objective grounds for confidence. Thus, whereas NATO was for long associated in people's minds with the post-war era of peace and prosperity, it now appears to many working-class voters as part and parcel of a system in which industry is being run down and unemployment is still rising, dependence on the United States is reaching unprecedented levels, and the gulf is widening between North and South of the country. An alternative to NATO, involving deep cuts in military spending, could allow more funds to be devoted to the struggle against unemployment, poverty and starvation at home and in the Third World, and to a radical programme of industrial regeneration in which new technologies are developed for social use rather than to erode trade union rights. As a major fiscal crisis looms in Britain, any government will be faced with a stark choice. Either the welfare state is shorn of finance in a way that makes recent cutbacks seem like a pin-prick; or the warfare state—the massive military-industrial complex—is drastically reduced in size and influence. It is no longer possible to continue sustaining the two at post-war levels, and it would be deceitful to tell the electorate otherwise.

It will also be necessary to address the understandable fear of some trade unionists that demilitarization will add to the acute problem of mass unemployment. 'Jobs not bombs' is not necessarily an attractive slogan to bomb-producers threatened with the dole queue. But although it is true that not every tank factory can be turned over to the production of medical equipment, years of research have demonstrated a tremendous potential for conversion from military to civilian use. Here too a nationally coordinated programme is urgently required, as well as provisions for the retraining of workers in the arms industry.

A third linkage that will carry considerable weight with labour-movement activists is the obvious, and far from accidental, coincidence of Cold War and anti-union drives by the Right. The recent period is no exception, as the US-led campaign to undermine the positions of organized labour spreads to one NATO country after another, with Britain once again in the forefront. There is even a special fund, as in the 1950s, to encourage the splitting of certain unions or the formation of rightist, anti-Communist currents in others.[66]

It will of course take time to effect a major change in public opinion on NATO, and the next general election is probably too close for this to break through as a central issue on the hustings. What is needed, in the short term, is the preparation of the Labour Party for a far-reaching debate in the period immediately following the next election. Such preliminary work would emphasize the entirely rational and sensible reasons for abandoning NATO, and provide the means and arguments for opinion to be changed. It would, too, consistently relate the issue of withdrawal to wider questions of peace and disarmament, posing it as a step to the break-up of military blocs. A policy of active non-alignment has nothing to do with 'Little England' mentalities, and while an appeal to follies of isolated grandeur might win votes in some quarters, it would exclude the British people from participation in the progressive internationalist currents that alone offer a hope for the survival of humanity. As the nuclear winter studies have grimly shown, not even Patagonian farmers or Arctic fishermen would be safe from the omnicidal effects of a strategic exchange of nuclear arsenals. The future of Britain is now, more than ever, bound up with that of the whole European continent, and any anti-NATO campaign here should make a strong priority of forging links with kindred forces throughout the world.[67]

In Conclusion

In 1983 the Turkish Peace Association argued that 'NATO, the Warsaw Pact, and indeed all other military pacts, will surely disappear', and asserted 'the inalienable right and duty of every Turkish intellectual to oppose military pacts and blocs'. In response the Turkish state charged TPA leaders with subversion and sentenced them to eight years' imprisonment for 'acting in accordance with the USSR to subvert freedom and democracy in the world, to wreck Turkey's alliances and pacts relating to the security of the Free World'.[68] This brutal repression occurred in a NATO country, because membership of the Alliance was challenged. It is a sobering reminder of what 'freedom and democracy' can mean for this military pact. In Turkey, to call for peaceful alternatives to it led to literal imprisonment. In Britain, it is mental imprisonment in the framework of Cold War thought that is the principal danger that faces us today. We hope and believe that this pamphlet, together with other serious work on the subject,[69] will contribute to a wide-ranging strategic debate that is long overdue in the labour and peace movements. If a government comes to power in the next two years with a commitment to anti-nuclear politics, we would urge it to adopt a policy of withdrawal from NATO and active non-alignment to ensure consistency in its defence and foreign policies. If, however, Labour remains in opposition, we would propose a campaign to persuade the Party that disengagement from the Atlantic Alliance is the most appropriate policy option and the one most likely to ensure an eventual return to power. Whichever development actually occurs, this text is put forward in the knowledge that NATO, like all alliances before it, must at some point cease to exist, and in the belief that the sooner it is replaced by a progressive, internationalist alternative, the safer this planet will be.

Notes

1. Harris poll conducted for ITN and reported on *Channel Four News*, 18 April 1986.
2. The *Guardian*, 17 March 1986.
3. The policy was most clearly outlined in Keynes's internal memorandum on 'Stage III' (the period following Germany's defeat), Public Record Office, CAB 65/66. Despite its rhetorical support for anti-colonialism, the US administration readily took advantage of British and other European possessions in the Pacific, the Middle East and Africa to set up bases and secure supplies of uranium and other raw materials.
4. See James E. Miller, 'Chaos or Christian Democracy. The ERP as a Factor in Italy's 1948 Elections', mimeo, Padua University.
5. The content of the discussions was only made available to the Western public thirty years later, but Moscow would have been immediately informed by its spy in the British delegation, Donald Maclean.
6. See Cees Wiebes and Bert Zeeman, 'The Pentagon Negotiations March 1948: The Launching of the North Atlantic Treaty', *International Affairs*, summer 1983.
7. For details of these plans, see David Alan Rosenberg, 'The Origins of Overkill', *International Security*, spring 1983.
8. 'Rollback' was first advocated in the US Government memorandum NSC 20/4 in late 1948, and hardened up in the wake of memorandum NSC 68 in 1950. See, for example, Rosenberg, p. 14. The actual documents can be found in *Foreign Relations of the United States* for the relevant years.
9. *Business Week*, 12 March 1979, pp. 40-1.
10. Quoted in R. Crossman, *Diaries of a Cabinet Minister*, vol. 1, London 1976, p. 95.
11. Resolution of the NATO Council meeting, 17 December 1952.
12. For details of NATO supplies to Portugal, which continued until its eventual defeat in Africa in 1974 – 75, see S.J. Borgia and C. van Krimpen, *Portugal and NATO*, Angola Comité, Amsterdam 1972.
13. Quoted in *Neue Zürcher Zeitung*, 2 March 1963.
14. See Ted Szulc, *The Illusion of Peace*, New York 1978, esp. p. 221.
15. *The Round Table*, July 1970.
16. British military strategists claim to have persuaded the Americans to adopt 'massive retailiation'. This is probably little more than an idle boast, but it does show how belligerent was British military policy at the time.
17. A useful source for details of such incidents is the American Friends Service Committee publication, *The Deadly Connection: Nuclear War and US Intervention*, Cambridge, Mass., 1983. Full sources can be found in B. Lowe, *The NATO Hot Potato*, Zed Press, forthcoming. See also Barry M. Blechman and

Stephen S. Kaplan, *Force Without War*, Brookings Institution, Washington 1978.

18. The December 1953 US defence programme identified 'the provision of tactical atomic support for US or allied military forces in general war or in a local aggression' as a major component of US military policy: Rosenberg, op. cit, p. 31.

19. See, for example, George W. Rathgens, Jr, 'NATO Strategy, Total War', in K. Knorr, ed., *NATO and American Security*, Princeton U.P. 1959.

20. Soviet leaders kept open the 'first use' option for much of the nuclear era, but have explicitly renounced it on various occasions since 1982. See, for example, the annual *Military Review* of the International Institute for Strategic Studies.

21. Quoted in Richard Barnet, *The Alliance*, New York 1983, p. 231.

22. Nevertheless, in the macabre planning that went on inside NATO, US military involvement was never fully guaranteed. See Alva Myrdal, 'The Superpowers' Game over Europe', in Thompson and Smith, eds., *Protest and Survive*, Harmondsworth 1980, pp. 95-7, 102-3.

23. For details of the hawks' campaigns and arguments on the nuclear question, see Jerry W. Sanders, *Peddlars of Crisis*, London 1983.

24. See J. Kolko and G. Kolko, *The Limits of Power*, New York 1972, p. 499.

25. Denis Healey, in a Fabian lecture, 26 November 1985. Healey has since explained that he does fear war might break out as a result of uprisings in Eastern Europe or a war in the Persian Gulf resulting from a US intervention and a Soviet counter-response. *Marxism Today*, April 1986, pp. 25-6.

26. See M.A. Evangelista, 'Stalin's Postwar Army Reappraised', *International Security*, winter 1982 – 83, vol. 7 no. 3.

27. See, for example, the annual *Military Review*, op. cit.

28. See 'The USSR and NATO', in K. Knorr, ed., op. cit., pp. 43-4.

29. The CIA helped to organise coups in Greece (1967) and Turkey (1971 and 1980). CIA agents were also involved in attempts to destabilize Portugal in 1974 – 6 and Italy in 1969 – 70.

30. David P. Calleo and Benjamin M. Rowland, *America and the World Political Economy*, Indiana University Press, 1973, pp. 45-6.

31. See the revelations of former MI5 agent Cathy Messiter, on *20/20 Vision*, Channel Four.

32. Quoted in Andy Thomas and Ben Lowe, *How Britain Was Sold*, Peace News pamphlet, p. 4.

33. Internal paper from Western Department of the Foreign Office, 4 January 1950, cited in ibid., p. 9.

34. For a selection of examples, see Duncan Campbell, *The Unsinkable Aircraft Carrier*, London 1984, pp. 301-2. The US troop presence has increased from 24,000 to 32,000 since the early 1950s—more than 8,000 being added between 1980 and 1986 as a result of the deployment of cruise missiles and

new aircraft designed either for espionage (TR1s) or for evading Soviet radar detection (EF-111s). See *Hansard*, 7 February 1986.

35. See the two articles by Patrick Forbes and Duncan Campbell in the *New Statesman*, 6 and 13 September 1985.

36. On Vietnam, see R. Barnet, op. cit., p. 158. On the Lebanon, see R.J. Spiller, 'Not War but Like War', *The American Intervention in the Lebanon*, Combat Studies Institute, 1981. On the October War incident, see for example, B.M. Blechman and D.M. Hart, 'The Political Utility of Nuclear Weapons, The 1973 Middle East Crisis', in *International Security*, Summer 1982.

37. See, for example, S. Menaul, *Countdown: Britain's Strategic Nuclear Forces*, London 1980, pp. 114-17. According to Dean Acheson, the US intention was to 'inform' not consult its allies: Barnet, op. cit., p. 232.

38. The French Parliament firmly rejected the idea of a European Defence Force that would include West Germany but not Britain.

39. See 'Rethink on the Rhine', The *Times*, 17 August 1983.

40. See, e.g., Lord Hill-Norton, 'Return to a National Strategy', in J. Baylis, ed., *Alternative Approaches to British Defence Policy*, London 1983, p. 122.

41. See Paul Rogers, 'A Note on UK Naval Deployments in the Falklands', *Peace Studies Briefings*, No. 14.

42. The notorious Exocet has a range of 30kms, but the Soviet Union has countless missiles of equivalent or superior technology with a range of 400kms. This may soon increase to 1000kms. See Lord Cameron, 'Alternative Strategies: Strategy, Tactics and New Technology', in Baylis, ed., p. 110.

43. For full details of this underwater detection system, called SOSUS, see Duncan Campbell, *The Unsinkable Aircraft Carrier*, pp. 171-4.

44. Whitehall retains the possibility of independent Polaris targeting, as was shown during the Falklands War. See the *New Statesman*, 15 February 1985.

45. Alliance plans for Out of Area activities have been devised by NATO's secret South West Asia Impact Study. For details, see the North Atlantic Assembly report on 'Out of Area Challenges to the Alliance', November 1983.

46. At its most modest, the SDI is designed to protect missiles and related communications facilities in the US. Few bar the President continue to believe in a total defence of US territory.

47. A *Newsweek* poll conducted in September 1985.

48. Simon Lunn, *Burden-Sharing in NATO*, Royal Institute of International Affairs, 1983, p. 6.

49. See, for example, the report of Fred Ikle's comments on the new Command to integrate space force with America's global air, army and naval forces—both conventional and nuclear—in E.P. Thompson, 'Folly's Comet', in Thompson, ed., *Star Wars*, Harmondsworth 1985, p. 124.

50. 'A Plan to Reshape NATO', *Time*, 5 March 1984, p. 14.

51. Labour shadow ministers, cited in the *Times*, 28 October 1985, p. 1.

52. *The Unsinkable Aircraft Carrier*, op. cit., pp. 255-7, 286-94.
53. A Harris poll for Channel 4 News put support for closure of all bases at 42% in the first week after the attack. If one includes 'don't knows', Labour's level of support in the polls is around 30%.
54. For the former view, see inter alia Strobe Talbot, *Deadly Gambits*, London 1985, pp. 33, 44.
55. See the comment to this effect by Sir David Scott, a senior civil servant who bore some responsibility for the initial decision to opt for Trident. The *Observer*, 6 March 1986.
56. See, for example, the remark by Lord Carrington reported in John Palmer, 'Sticky Paper, or Policies to Patch Up NATO's Cracks', The *Guardian*, 4 October 1985.
57. Interview in *Marxism Today*, April 1986, p. 28.
58. *Labour and World Society*, p. 9.
59. Within NATO itself, elected governments have been overthrown in Greece (1967) and Turkey (1960, 1971 and 1980).
60. See, for example, the *Guardian*, 20 November 1985.
61. Poll for *News on Sunday*, by RSGB Ltd.
62. *Social Attitudes*, 1985, p. 102.
63. See Dan Plesch, 'Airland Battle and NATO's Military Posture', *ADIU Report*, vol. 7. no. 2, March – April 1985, and all references cited therein.
64. For example, leaders of the TGWU, AUEW – TASS and NUM.
65. For a discussion of the European dimension, see in particular Fred Halliday, *The Making of the Second Cold War*, 2nd edn., Verso, London 1986.
66. For full details, see *International Labour Reports*, January-February 1986.
67. The 1986 congress of the SPD, combined with the presence of the Greens, confirmed the vitality of anti-hegemonist peace currents among the German population. No doubt this will be one of the most important openings for international collaboration in the next few years.
68. Quoted in M.A. Dikerdem, *Turkey's Peace Trials*, pamphlet. The leaders of the TPA had all been highly respected members of the Turkish establishment. After an intensive international campaign, the last of those imprisoned was released in early 1986.
69. See especially Jonathan Steele et al., *The Politics of Alternative Defence*, forthcoming, Grafton Books. Although the authors advance a more gradual approach than the one contained in this pamphlet, they have made a most welcome contribution that should be widely read and discussed.

Peace Through Non-Alignment

After the raid on Libya in April 1986, many people in Britain expressed alarm and fury that American bases could be used to launch an attack on a third country and that the British Government was apparently powerless to act in the face of the aggressive demands of an American President.

As a result of this anger a large number of peace organisations came together, originally to organise demonstrations to show their horror and disgust at what Mrs Thatcher had done. Later, on 15th July, the Campaign Group of Labour MPs took an initiative to form a Campaign for Non-Alignment for Great Britain in the future, and this was attended by a number of Labour MPs and representatives of a variety of peace and internationalist bodies.

Many people spoke at this meeting and expressed support for the concept of a campaign which would link together the obvious dangers of American bases in Great Britain; the threat of yet more nuclear weapons; and the looming crisis for the world's poorest people by the process of debt collection resulting in starvation.

Those present were supportive of the view that a campaign was necessary which would:

(a) Redirect British policy towards the active promotion of international peace and disarmament;
(b) Divert resources from military expenditure towards peaceful development here and in the Third World;
(c) Co-operate with the non-aligned countries in their policies for development and disarmament;
(d) Maintain support for the popular movements struggling for independence, human rights and democracy;
(e) Support the United Nations;
(f) Secure the withdrawal of all American bases and forces from Britain and all the territories; and
(g) Disengage Britain from NATO.

This group then elected a steering committee, who are organising a major conference to be held in London on 24th January 1987 to promote peace through non-alignment.

For further information on this campaign, please write to the Campaign for Non-Alignment, c/o Jeremy Corbyn MP, Red Rose Centre, 129 Seven Sisters Road, London N7 7QG.

Campaign Group Pamphlets

Published by Verso

A Million Jobs a Year

A Case for Planning Full Employment
Andrew Glynn

Economist Andrew Glyn outlines the steps that would be necessary
for a future Labour government to tackle seriously the problem
of unemployment.

40 pages

£1.50   ISBN 0 86091 838 6

Justice

The Miners' Strike 1984-5

Dennis Skinner, Tony Benn, Bob Clay, Bill Etherington, Marina
Lewycka, Alan Meale, Paul Stanley and Roger Windsor.

This illustrated pamphlet outlines the history of the miners'
magnificent strike and analyses the Tories' attacks on the NUM
through the courts, police force and sequestrators.

64 pages

£1.95   ISBN 0 86091 999 4

Available from your local bookseller or direct from:
Verso, 6 Meard Street, London W1.

VERSO

SUBSCRIBE TO
Campaign Group News

Campaign Group News is a paper for left activists in the party. It plays a unique role in supporting the efforts of campaigning organisations like Labour CND, the Labour Women's Action Committee, the Campaign for Labour Party Democracy, the Labour Party Black Section, the Justice for Mineworkers' Campaign, the Labour Campaign for Lesbian and Gay Rights and the Labour Committee on Ireland.

Campaign Group News provides to the membership of the party a record of the activities of the NEC and PLP which is not available anywhere else.

Campaign Group News unambiguously opposes all witch hunts and violations of democracy within the party.

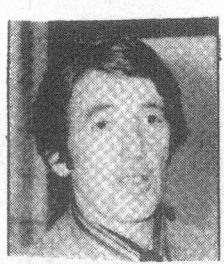

Tony Benn MP

'Campaign Group News exists to give radical forces on the left a voice.'

Dennis Skinner MP

'Campaign Group News is the paper for comrades who want to find out what really happens in the NEC and PLP.'

Subscribe to Campaign Group News

Individual subscriptions rate: One year £5.
Bulk rates are 20 pence per copy for 10 copies or more.
Supporting subscribers' rate: One year £10.

Name . . . .

Address . . . .

. . . . Telephone . . . .

For bulk orders specify quantity . . . .

Make all cheques payable to Campaign Group News.
Send completed form to: The Campaign Group of Labour MPs, c/o Alan Meale (Secretary), House of Commons, London SW1A OAA.

Printed and bound by CPI Group (UK) Ltd, Croydon, CR0 4YY

06/05/2026

02103654-0003